Belwin Piano Method

IN FIVE BOOKS

Dear Friends:

You are now beginning Book Two of the Belwin Piano Method. In this book you will continue to plan fingerings and to write finger numbers in the boxes that have been included for that purpose. You will find this program of finger planning a great aid to reading as well as to technical efficiency. Again, as in Book One, the back cover contains a summary of the information which is presented in this book.

The five books of this Method are designed for anyone from school age through adult — hood. In all of the books, from the early grade material of Book One through the introduction to Contemporary in Book Five, we think that you will enjoy and profit by the "MUSICAL MUSIC" that is offered to you.

Best wishes to you.

Sincerely,

June Weybright

Author, Belwin Piano Method

CONTENTS

Etude

Etude is a French word meaning a Study or Exercise. The ETUDE below is a study in note reading and finger planning. In the six small boxes that are drawn above and below the notes, write the numbers of the fingers that you plan to use.

The dotted lines in the third line of the piece indicate that the melody alternates between the two hands.

An Etude

Plan the fingering

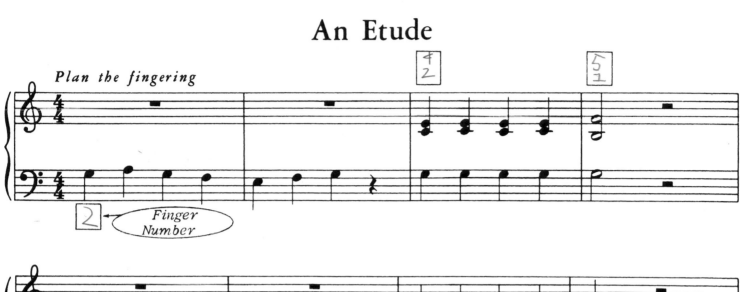

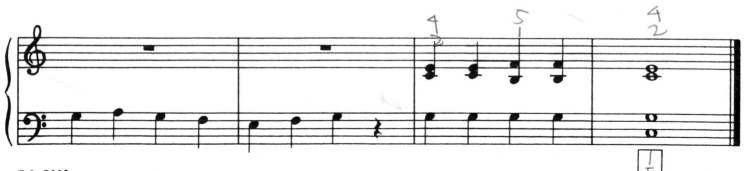

E.L.2006

4

Finger Planning

Continue to write finger numbers in the boxes that you will find above and below notes throughout this book.

Sailing Along

Sailing along in the moonlight,
Sailing along through the night.

KEY SIGNATURE
F#

Play smoothly

First F#

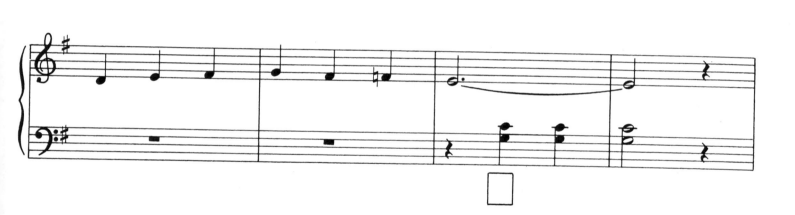

E.L.2006

6

Ring, Ring the Banjo

Stephen Foster

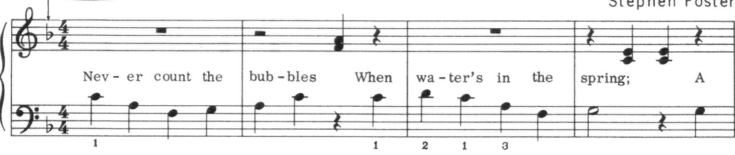

KEY SIGNATURE Bb

Nev - er count the bub - bles When wa - ter's in the spring; A

fel - low's got no trou - bles While there's a song to sing.

First Bb

Ring, ring the ban - jo! I like that good old song,

Come a - gain my true love, Where have you been so long?

Technic

TECHNIC is the mechanical skill of playing.
Practicing technic studies helps to produce that skill.

Keep a good hand position at the keyboard.

Technic Studies
for
Right Hand

for
Left Hand

for
Both Hands

Suggestion for Supplementary writing material:
   BELWIN THEORY WORKSHEETS by JUNE WEYBRIGHT - Set No. Two

E.L.2006

8

Folk music of the various countries of the world differs in character just as the people of various nations differ from each other. Polish folk music expresses the vigor and spirit of the Polish people.

Poland gave to the world two of its greatest musicians, Chopin and Paderewski.

A Polish Folk Song

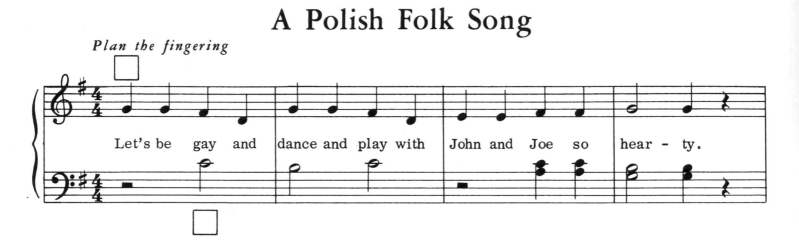

Let's be gay and dance and play with John and Joe so hear - ty.

Here's to joy for girl and boy and health to all the par - ty.

Tone Shading

Tone shading is the rise and fall in the volume of sound that makes music interesting. It is often referred to as Expression.

Many tone shading directions are Italian words that have been used since music writing started in Italy about the year 1,000.

The following shading terms are used in A QUESTION –

FORTE (loud)   PIANO (soft)

A Question

Shading terms are often abbreviated.

f   (forte)

p   (piano)

The Jasmine Flower

Chinese Folk Song

Opera

An opera is a play set to music, a kind of music drama. In grand opera every word is sung but in light opera some of the lines are spoken.

FAUST is a grand opera written by the French composer, Charles Gounod, and first presented in Paris in 1859. Its continued popularity is due to its excellent music.

Ballet Music
from
Faust

Mezzo forte (mf) medium loud

Charles Gounod

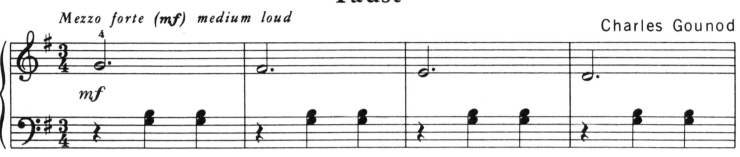

E.L.2006

*When repeating play **p** (piano)*

This carol tells of Good King Wenzel, who was King of Bohemia in the first century from the year 928 to 935. His good deeds to poor people were known throughout his land.

Good King Wenceslas

John Neal

Old Carol

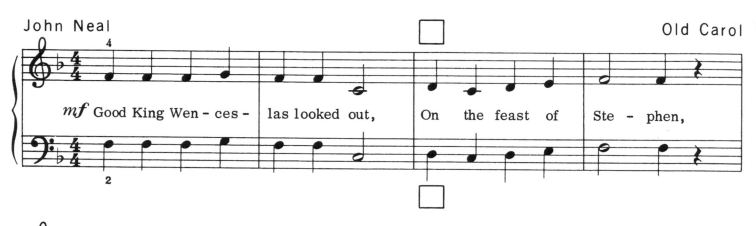

mf Good King Wen - ces - las looked out, On the feast of Ste - phen,

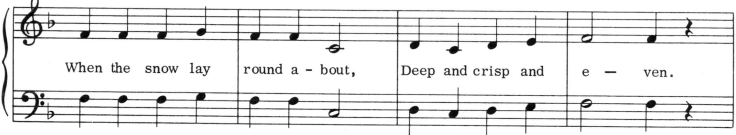

When the snow lay round a - bout, Deep and crisp and e — ven.

Bright-ly shone the moon that night, Though the frost was cru — el,

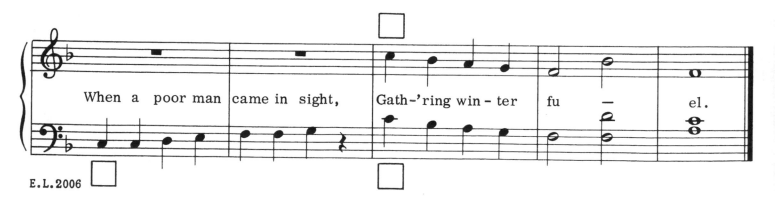

When a poor man came in sight, Gath-'ring win - ter fu — el.

E.L.2006

Accidentals

Occasional flats, naturals and sharps, aside from those included in the key signature, are called ACCIDENTALS.

There are accidentals in the second and fourth lines of WINTER ADIEU.

Winter Adieu

Mezzo piano (mp) medium soft

A German Folk Song

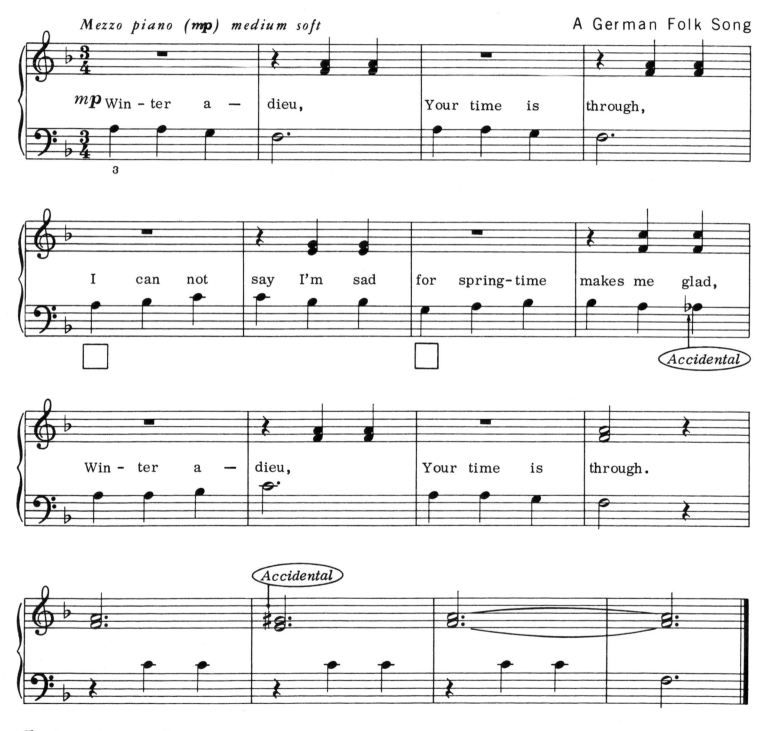

Sheet music suggestion:
   EXCERPTS from TWO STRAUSS WALTZES - arr. by JUNE WEYBRIGHT

E.L.2006

An accidental is in effect for one measure unless cancelled by another sign.

At the new measure, the accidental must be repeated if it is to be continued.

Minka

With vigor

A Russian Folk Song

Even though an accidental is in effect for one measure only, a sign cancelling it is often written in the new measure as a reminder that the accidental has ended.

Such reminder signs are written in the last measures of the second and fourth lines of SWANEE RIVER.

Swanee River

Plan the fingering

Stephen Foster

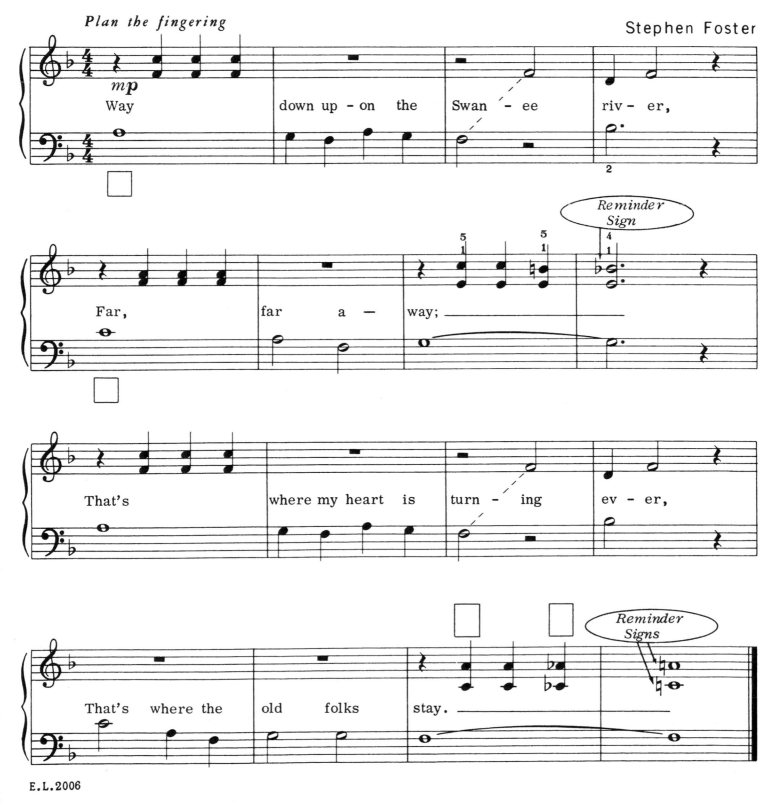

The Damper Pedal

The DAMPER PEDAL (the one on the right) sustains and enriches tones. With your right foot, press down and release the damper pedal several times to acquaint yourself with the feel of it.

A Pedal Mark

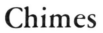

Down   *Up*

The above mark, written under the staff, shows when pedal is to be used.   Press it down at the beginning of the mark and release it at the end.

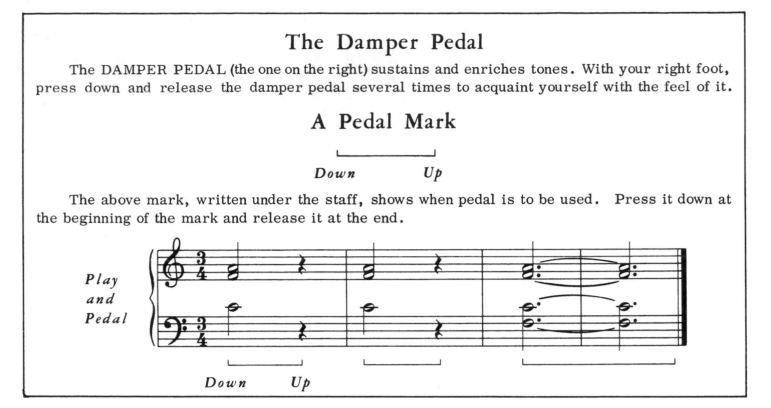

Play and Pedal

Down   Up

Chimes

Pedal as Marked

mf

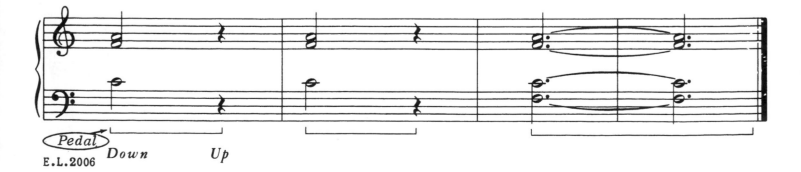

Pedal Down   Up

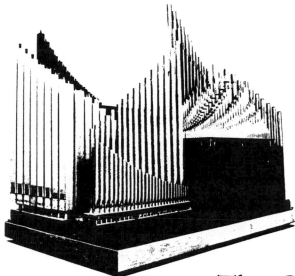

The Organ

The organ is an instrument in which the sound is made by pipes of different sizes and blown by wind pressure.

The first church organ was made in the first century. Both the Germans and the English excelled in organ building in the early days. The first American organ, played by electric power, was built in 1876.

Today, the electronic organ, which has no pipes has become very popular.

The Organ Plays

Slowly

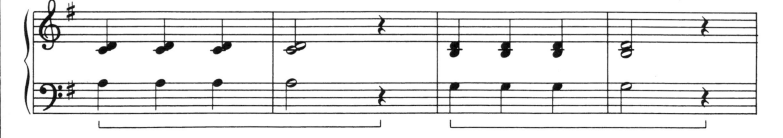

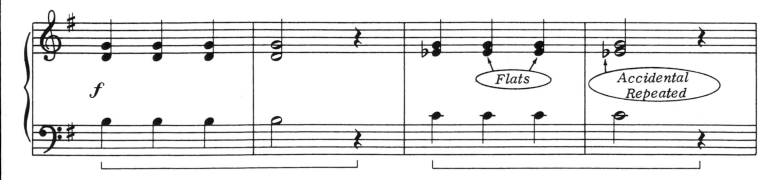

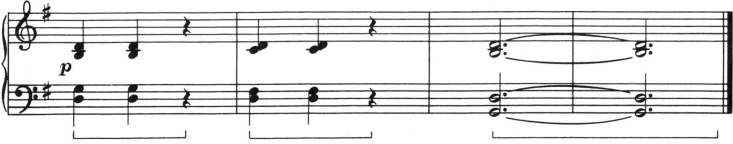

Sheet music suggestion for additional Pedal practice:
BLEST BE THE TIE THAT BINDS – arr. by JUNE WEYBRIGHT

E.L. 2006

Johann Strauss, Jr.

Johann Strauss, Jr. was a member of a famous Austrian family of composers. He was born in Vienna in 1825 and became known as the WALTZ KING because of the grace and beauty of his many dance compositions. He was widely known as a conductor and, through his orchestral concerts, he brought the gaiety of Old Vienna to all Europe and, later, to America.

Some of his most familiar compositions are BEAUTIFUL BLUE DANUBE, TALES OF THE VIENNA WOODS, ARTIST'S LIFE and DIE FLEDERMAUS.

Roses from the South

Gracefully

Johann Strauss. Jr.

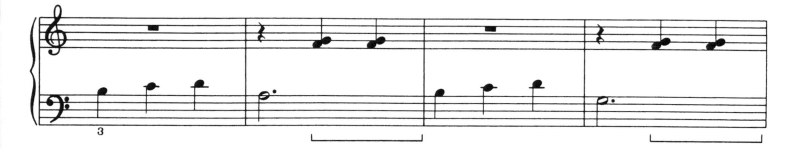

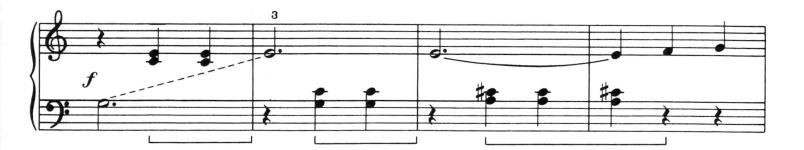

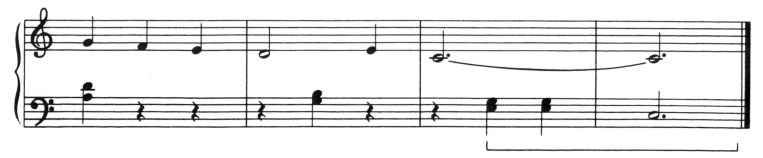

Sheet music suggestion for the Younger Student:
NONSENSE SONG by JUNE WEYBRIGHT

E.L.2006

A Time Table
of
Note and Rest Values

The following are the notes and rests that you have played thus far —

Notes		Rests		Values
♩ -	Quarter	𝄽 -	Quarter	1 beat
♩ -	Half	▬ -	Half	2 beats
♩. -	Dotted Half			3 beats
𝅝 -	Whole	▬ -	Whole	4 beats

Eighth Notes
A New Value

♫ — TWO EIGHTH NOTES are worth one beat.

In order to fit two eighth notes to each beat, they must be played TWICE AS FAST AS QUARTER NOTES.

Tapping Exercise

Count aloud and tap the notes below. Be sure that every beat is EXACTLY THE SAME LENGTH.

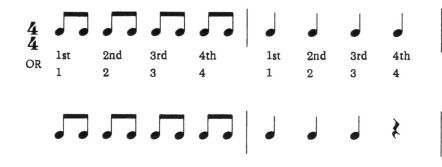

Suggestion

Before reading the entire EIGHTH NOTE STUDY below, play the left hand of the first line many times until it is well learned.

By doing this, you will be able to play the eighth notes twice as fast as the quarters with ease.

Eighth Note Study

Groups of eighth notes are often printed together thus - ♪♪♪♪ . This does not change their value. Continue to play them twice as fast as quarter notes.

Summer

Smoothly

mf

Pleas-ant are the days in sum - mer, Pleas-ant are the night times too.

Four Eighth Notes

♪ - This is one eighth note.   𝄾 - This is an eighth rest.

You will find single eighth notes and rests in the TECHNIC STUDIES below.
(Eighth rests have the same value as eighth notes.)

Technic Studies
for
Right Hand

for
Left Hand

for
Both Hands

Tempo

TEMPO is an Italian word meaning the rate of speed of the music.

Words directing tempo are written at the beginning of a piece.

Arkansas Traveller

Moderato (Moderate tempo)

Early American Song

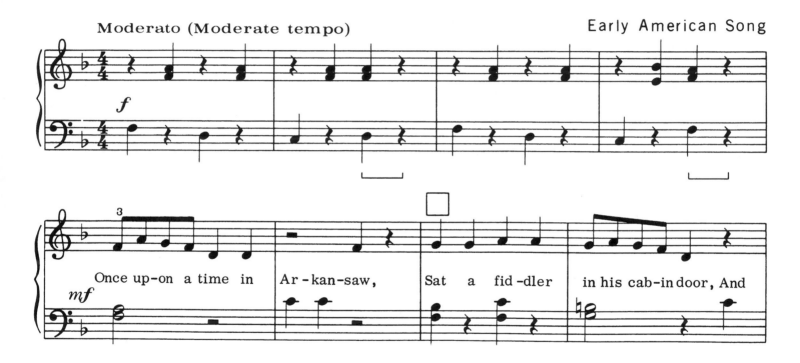

Once up-on a time in Ar-kan-saw, Sat a fid-dler in his cab-in door, And

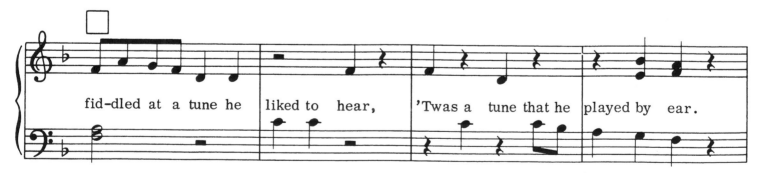

fid-dled at a tune he liked to hear, 'Twas a tune that he played by ear.

The key signature of VESPER BELLS is two flats (B♭ and E♭). There are many B's and E's in this piece. Flat them all.

Vesper Bells

A Folk Song

Hark! the ves-per hymn is ring-ing, Loud and clear the mu - sic swells;

While on sum - mer breez-es gent-ly wing-ing Comes the mel-low chime of

ves - per bells.

26

Jaques Offenbach

Jacques Offenbach, who lived from 1819 to 1880, was the first great composer of French comic opera. Within a twenty five year period he composed nearly ninety such works.

In his sparkling and witty opera, ORPHEUS IN THE UNDERWORLD, Offenbach introduced the CANCAN which was a popular dance in the late nineteenth century.

The Cancan

E.L.2006

An accent (>) means to play with special emphasis.

Igor Stravinsky

Igor Stravinsky is a great composer of the present day. Among his many works are several well known ballets. A ballet is a play which is performed by dancers with costumes, scenery and music but without singing or speaking parts.

Stravinsky's ballet, THE FIREBIRD, caused a great sensation when it was first produced in Paris in 1910 and has never lost its popularity. His PETROUCHKA and THE RITE OF SPRING have enjoyed equal success.

Dance of the Princesses
from
The Firebird

Moderate tempo and very smoothly

Igor Stravinsky

E.L.2006

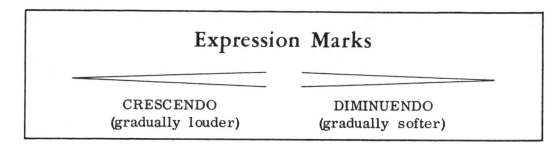

Expression Marks

CRESCENDO
(gradually louder)

DIMINUENDO
(gradually softer)

Through the Trees

Winds go pushing through the trees,
Winds that no one ever sees.

Allegretto (Moderately quick)

Sheet music suggestion for Additional Eighth Note Study:
SCANDINAVIAN DANCE SONG – arr. by JUNE WEYBRIGHT

E.L. 2006

The Fifth Finger

A strong fifth finger helps to make a good hand position. Play FINGER FIVE on its tip and straight down to the key.

Technic Studies

for

Right Hand

for

Left Hand

Suggestion for Black Key Technic:

When repeating the above STUDIES, <u>sharp</u> <u>every</u> <u>note</u>.

The key signature of THE HARP is two sharps (F♯ and C♯). There are several F's and C's to be sharped in this piece.

The fifth finger plays repeatedly in THE HARP and in REVEILLE on the opposite page. Keep a good fifth finger position always.

The Harp

C - The Imperfectum

A broken circle, called the IMPERFECTUM (C), often substitutes for a $\frac{4}{4}$ time signature.

Many hundreds of years ago it was believed that music with measures of three beats had the only perfect rhythm. Such music used an unbroken circle, called the PERFECTUM (O), for its time signature.

The Imperfectum has remained in use to the present day but the Perfectum has not.

Reveille

A Bugle Call

Suggestion: Repeat REVEILLE
and sharp every note.

D.C. al Fine
D.C. al Fine - repeat from the
beginning to Fine (the end)

E.L.2006

A New Pedal Mark

The damper pedal can be used to connect tones. The mark above indicates such a use.

PEDAL EXERCISE

1 - Press down the damper pedal with the right foot.
2 - By a quick motion of the foot, release and repress the pedal in ONE SINGLE ACTION. (This foot action will be referred to as a FLIP in the following exercise.)

PLAYING EXERCISE

1 - Without pedal, play the two measures below until they are learned.
2 - Then play again pressing down the pedal at the beginning of the pedal mark.
3 - Just before the arrow in the pedal mark (——^——), with the PEDAL STILL DOWN, place your hands in position over the new notes.
4 - Then PLAY THE NEW NOTES and FLIP THE PEDAL AT EXACTLY THE SAME TIME.

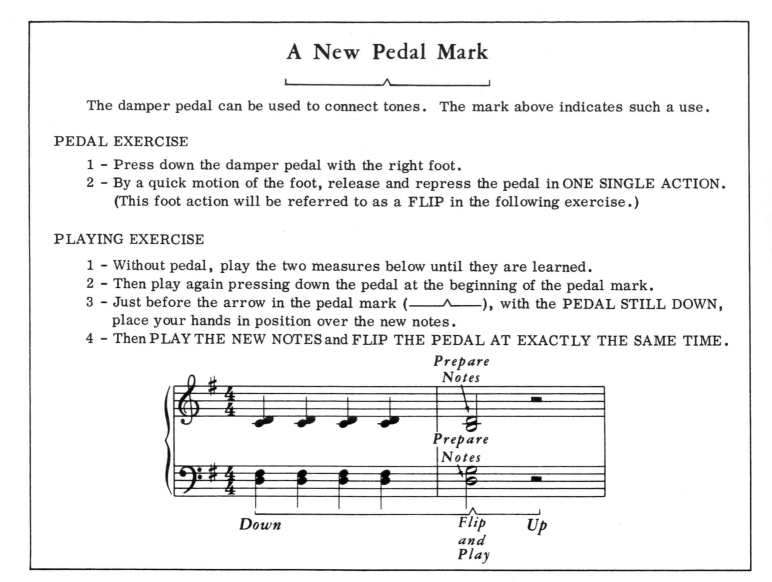

Voices from the Choir

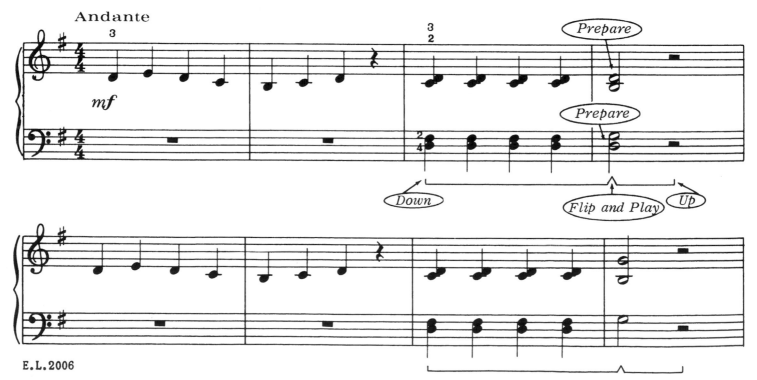

Sheet music suggestion for Additional Pedal Practice:

For the Younger Student – WALKING TO SCHOOL by JUNE WEYBRIGHT
For the Older Student – IN CHURCH by JUNE WEYBRIGHT

E.L.2006

The SKATER'S WALTZ, written by Emil Waldteufel, who lived from 1837 to 1915, has enjoyed as much popularity as the famous Strauss Waltzes.

Skaters' Waltz

Emil Waldteufel

Waltz tempo

A repeat sign placed at the beginning and at the end of a section of a piece means to repeat only the part between the signs.

Repeat
from sign

rit. ritard

Intervals and Chords

 An INTERVAL consists of two tones.

 A CHORD consists of three or more tones.

You have already played many intervals in your pieces. Now, in HUNGARIAN DANCE, you will play both intervals and chords.

Johannes Brahms

The music of Johannes Brahms, who lived from 1833 to 1897, is among the greatest in the world. He composed in every field of music except opera. His HUNGARIAN DANCES make fine use of Hungarian folk music.

Hungarian Dance
No. 5

Fine

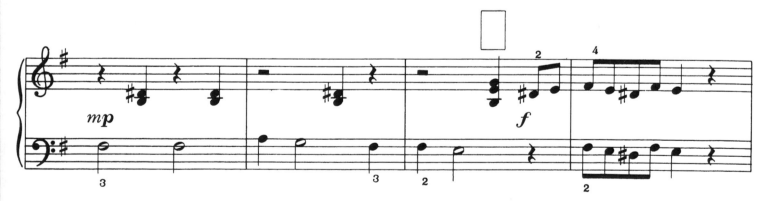

D.C. al Fine
Repeat from
beginning to Fine

Sheet music suggestion: BLUE DANUBE WALTZ - arr. by JUNE WEYBRIGHT

E.L.2006

The word scherzo indicates music of a light and pleasant character. This SCHERZO by the great Norwegian composer, Edvard Grieg, makes use of chords to accompany the melody.

Scherzo

Edvard Grieg

Interval Names

Intervals have number names thus:

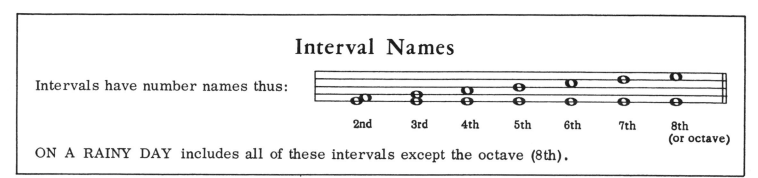

2nd 3rd 4th 5th 6th 7th 8th (or octave)

ON A RAINY DAY includes all of these intervals except the octave (8th).

On a Rainy Day

Sheet music suggestion: PRAYER by JUNE WEYBRIGHT

E.L.2006

Half Steps

From any key to the nearest key on either side is a HALF STEP. Examples of half steps are: C – C♯, E – F, B♭ – B♮, G – G♭, C – B.

Whole Steps

From any key to the second nearest key is a WHOLE STEP. Examples of whole steps are: C – D, E – F♯, B♭ – C, G – F, C – B♭.

Scales

A SCALE is a succession of rising pitches. There are many kinds of scales. Our basic scale is a diatonic scale made of the tones c d e f g a b c. It is called the C Major scale.

The C Major Scale

The C Major scale consists of whole and half steps in the following order:

Other Major Scales

A Major scale may be formed on any tone if the above pattern of whole and half steps is followed.

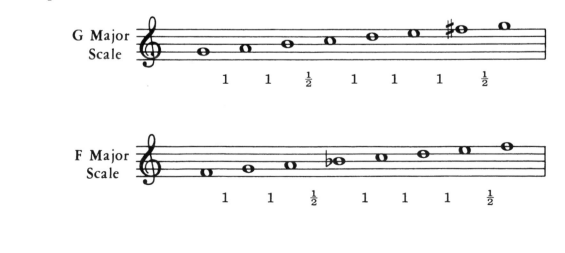

Scales are the tonal material out of which music is made. The SCALE STUDY below is made from the tones of the G Major scale.

Music that is based principally on the tones of a certain scale is in the key of that scale.

Thus, SCALE STUDY is in the KEY OF G MAJOR.

A Scale Study

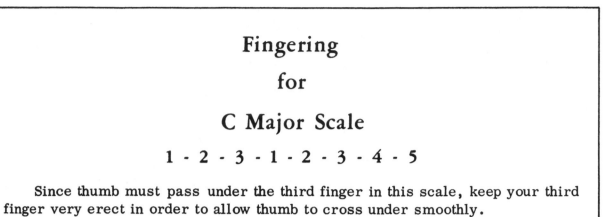

Fingering

for

C Major Scale

1 - 2 - 3 - 1 - 2 - 3 - 4 - 5

Since thumb must pass under the third finger in this scale, keep your third finger very erect in order to allow thumb to cross under smoothly.

Scale Technic

for

Right Hand

for

Left Hand

for

Both Hands

ETUDE IN C is so called because it is in the key of C Major.

Etude in C

Intervals *Scale* *Chords* *Repeat from here*

Fine

D.S. al Fine

D.S. al Fine means to repeat from this sign (𝄋) to Fine.

John Philip Sousa

John Philip Sousa, composer and conductor who was born in Washington D.C. in 1854 and died in 1932, was one of the most important figures in the history of American band music. His stirring compositions and his excellent leadership won for him the title of MARCH KING.

Some of his best known marches are SEMPER FIDELIS, STARS AND STRIPES FOREVER, WASHINGTON POST MARCH and EL CAPITAN.

Stars and Stripes Forever

John Philip Sousa

March tempo

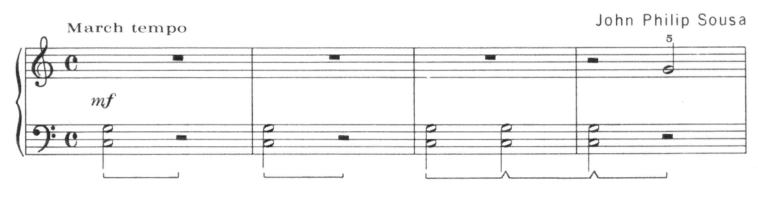

E.L.2006

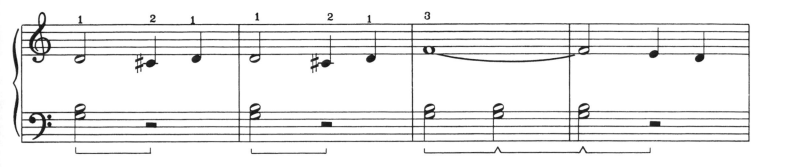

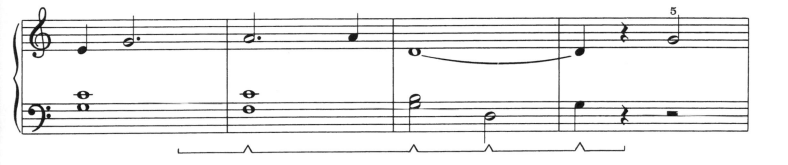

E.L.2006

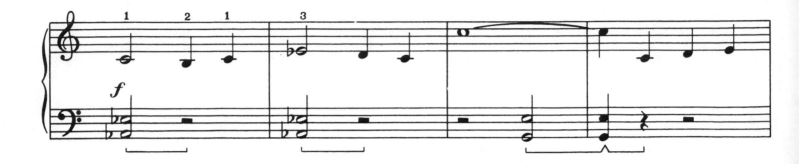

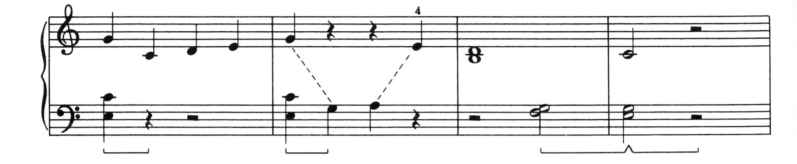

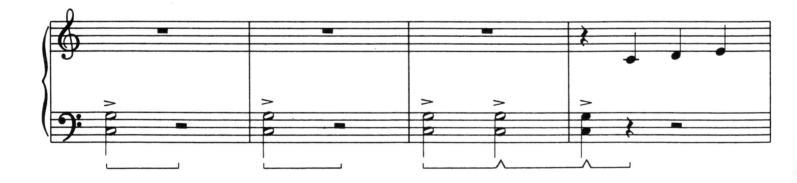

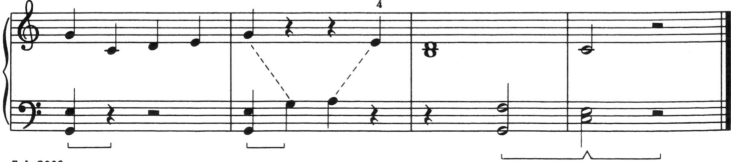

Certificate of Award

THIS IS TO CERTIFY THAT

_____

has completed

BOOK TWO
of the

Belwin Piano Method

by

June Weybright

and is now ready for

BOOK THREE

_____

Date

_____

Teacher

Summary

of

Information in Book Two

1 - Accidentals (see Pages 13, 14 and 15).

2 - Pedal, two uses (see Pages 16 and 32).

3 - Eighth note rhythms (see Pages 20 and 21).

4 - Tone shading terms —

Forte (*f*) - loud

Piano (*p*) - soft

Mezzo forte (*mf*) - moderately loud

Mezzo piano (*mp*) - moderately soft

Crescendo (*cresc.*) - gradually louder

Diminuendo (*dim.*) - gradually softer

- crescendo

- diminuendo

5 - Tempo (speed) terms —

Moderato - moderate tempo

Andante - moderately slow

Allegro - quick

Allegretto - moderately quick

Ritard (*rit.*) - gradually slower

A tempo - end ritard

6 - Signs —

D.C. al fine (Da capo al fine) - repeat from beginning to Fine (the end).

D.S. al fine (Dal segno al fine) - repeat from sign (𝄋) to the end.

— repeat the part between dots.

Imperfectum (**C**) - $\frac{4}{4}$ time signature

7 - Interval - two tones —

Names of Intervals (see Page 39).

8 - Chord — three or more tones.

9 - Half and Whole steps (see Page 40).

10 - Scale - a succession of rising pitches.

11 - Major scale pattern (see Page 40).

12 - Types of music in Book Two —

Etude, Carol, Folk Song, Opera, Waltz, March, Ballet.